# Christian Dream Interpretation

*Christian Dream Dictionary*

*Revised Edition*

Copyright © 2013 Brenda McDonald

# Christian Dream Interpretation

## Christian Dream Dictionary

### Revised Edition

ISBN-13: 978-1484925423

ISBN-10: 1484925424

# ACKNOWLEDGMENTS

I thank the loving group of my dearest friends and dedicated intercessors who have prayed diligently into my life and ministry. Thank you my Jesus for sending me your precious servants who have surrendered into Your Love.

# CONTENTS

# Introduction

It is with great joy that I am empowered to write this book.

My heart is to see you, the reader, move into a realm of supernatural understanding and interpretation of your dreams. I pray that this book of dream symbols will bring you into a new dimension of God, that will draw you even closer to His heart. In that closeness and intimacy with Him

comes all revelation, understanding and council.

Many years ago as I began to receive revelation about my own dreams, I sought the Lord for a deeper understanding into His nighttime parables. Holy Spirit honored my hunger by beginning to reveal the hidden meanings. I remain hungry even now as the Lord continues to teach and guide through dream encounters of the heavenly kind.

We know that through the history of Biblical examples God will speak to His people in parabolic type and symbols.

One third of the bible is about this type of communication from God.

For instance, Jacob received his greatest blessing and revelation of his future in a dream. A **ladder**, coming from the heavenly realm into the earth where the angels ascended and descended. The **ladder**, representing the **portal** into the heavens. God blessed Jacob with a hope and a future, as He spoke to him.

This form of communication is very important to God and He will give us the understanding as we seek His interpretation of our dreams. The Holy Spirit is the Spirit of Truth, and ultimately all God interpretation will come through Him. The Holy Spirit will bear witness in our spirit and we will know the truth of what God is saying to us in our dreams.

It is my prayer that these symbols within these pages will serve as a *catalyst* to propel you into the supernatural gift of interpretation.

May the Lord Jesus be glorified in your life.

You are being given "Keys to the Kingdom" of God within these pages. Grow into more of His understanding. May the blessing and enrichment of the Holy Spirit let my ceiling become your floor!

May the Spirit of the Lord increase your

understanding as you read and consume this book. May you have an insatiable hunger for the Word of God in your life.

May faith in God provide you with spiritual eyes and ears to hear and see what the Lord is revealing to you.

We are born again by grace through faith. Let our faith enable us to see what God is saying.

**Ephesians 1:17 Amplified Bible**

"[For I always pray to] the God **of** our Lord Jesus Christ, the Father **of** glory, that He may grant you a **spirit of** wisdom and **revelation** [of insight into mysteries and secrets] in the [deep and intimate] knowledge **of** Him."

# 1
# ANIMALS/INSECTS

Consider if the animal is a pet, domestic, tamed or wild. How does the presence of that animal make you feel? Animals may represent how others are acting toward us. They may also represent how we are acting. It may represent a danger or a blessing coming.

1. **Alligators/Hippos** – Someone opening a 'big mouth' against you. Stealthy and dangerous.
2. **Ants** – Wisdom, store things for the future. Industrious. Organized. Purpose oriented.
3. **Bats** – Spirit of delusion and self-righteous. Night creatures. Demonic.
4. **Bears-** A fierce attack, a cunning and sneaky predator that hunts 18 hours a day.
   **White Bears** – death to self; righteousness.
   **Brown Bears** – fear of the Lord. Cursing as in the destroyer bears of Elisha. **Black Bear** fear of man. Russia. Bear market. Evil man. Danger. Pillager. Hunter.
5. **Bees** – curses, chastisement, stings of hurt and pain by someone's words or actions. Too busy, or "busy as a bee". Negative – demonic

attack. Positive is community, honey and cross-pollinating.

6. **Butterfly** –Change, freedom, metamorphosis. Change brings beauty. Cross-pollinating.

7. **Birds** – confusion, wrong message. The Holy Spirit Dove is a good meaning. Birds singing joy, peace ,love, also harmony and unity. Dead birds are gloom and sorrow, heavy emotional burdens coming. Curses and the demonic are represented by birds also. Hatching birds, new beginnings, new friends, new business or relationships that will require some effort to grow it up.

8. **Black Bird**- curse or misfortune. A bad sign. Lack of motivation or using your full potential. If the bird is flying away may be good for you and the bad times are over now.

9. **Blue Bird-** is revelation. Blue birds are happiness or joy. Good news coming your way.

10. **Camel-** Provision. Water carrier.

11. **Caterpillar-**Destructive powers.

12. **Centipede** – ancient generations.

13. **Cock Roaches** – demons

14. **Cows** – Provision. Milk, the milk of the Word. Meat, the meat of the Word. Neg. "Golden Calf" – an idol that needs to be removed.

15. **Crab**-hard shell difficult to be near. Climbs on

the backs of others to get to a higher place. Moves sideways instead of forward.

16. **Crows** – mockers and harassers.(Negative) Fed God's prophet also.(Positive)

17. **Dragon**- The devel.

18. **Deer**-Timid, graceful. (eyes that allure as in Jezebel)

19. **Dog** – Contention, unclean spirits. Note: recognize how dog's attitude is; friendly, mean, aggressive, etc. The color of the dog is important as well. (see colors). Example **Black dog** – strong spirit of unbelief. **White Dog**- Purity, faith etc. Consider how you feel about a particular breed of dog.(Pos. or Neg.)Does the dog bring fear or bring comfort?

20. **Doves** – Holy Spirit. Peace. Weeping intercessor. Messengers. Mourning. (Also is the same as a pigeon)

21. **Eagles** – prophetic. Consider color. White eagle-Moving in pure revelation, gray eagle-moving in mixture. (Gray eagle uses gray matter or brain more than spirit) United States. Keen eyes. Prophet.

22. **Elephants** – wisdom, strength, long memory. Neg. – persecution.

23. **Frogs**-unclean spirits, evil, plague

24. **Flamingo** – Instruments that carry out Gods purpose.

25. **Fish** – Humanity. Men. Evangelism. Provision. Newly saved.

26. **Fly** – Beelzebub. Spirit of witchcraft. Spoils the oil. Pollute. Feeds on dead things.

27. **Form of an Animal** – looks like an animal, but is transparent – spiritual issues being revealed.

28. **Geese** – Watchman on the walls. Intercessors.

29. **Gnat/Mosquito** – witchcraft

30. **Goat**-Sinners. Sin.

31. **Hippos** – 'Water horses' – someone who is moving in the Spirit, but who's carnal nature is in control.

32. **Horses** –**White horses** – the Holy Spirit. **Black horse** – spirit of famine. **Pale Horse**-Spirit of Death and pestilence. **Red Horse**-Spirit of war.

33. **Leopard**- predator, dangerous, terrorist. Loner, dishonest.

34. **Mice or Rats** – thoughts and works of the mind. Unclean things. They get into 'cracks' and inside walls. Destruction.

35. **Monkeys** – Mischief, harassers as in; 'monkey on your back'. Dishonesty. Foolishness. Mocking.

36. **Mosquitos**- brings disease. Blood suckers. Pests

37. **Moths** – destroy cloths

38. **Mountain Lion** – Unavoidable problems.
39. **Owls** – Wisdom. White owls – pure wisdom from God. Negative – lonely or solitary. Night hunter.
40. **Oxen** – symbol of a rich sacrifice. Worker. Servantude.
41. **Lamb-** baby Christian. Believers.
42. **Lion** – Lion of Judah, Kingship, royalty. Strength, boldness of courage. Good and evil.
43. **Panther** (black) – predator, cunning, sneaky, coming for someone. Witchcraft. Someone is authority or high position trying to dishonor you or gobble up your reputation.
44. **Pelican-** Lonely or solitary person.
45. **Phoenix** – Resurrection power. Rising from the ashes of repentance.
46. **Pigs** – Real messy situation. Unclean, not kosher. Delivered from a demonic activity that is messy.

47. **Rabbits** – destruction
48. **Rat-** Deceiver. Carries disease. Scoundrel. Good for nothing. Traitor. Cheat or crook. Wrong thinking.
49. **Rooster-** wake up call. Betrayal. New morning, new mercies. Fertile.
50. **Sands-**humanity, physical.
51. **Scorpions** – Black magic/witchcraft. White scorpion – white witchcraft. Sickness.

52. **Shark-** Oppression. Spiritual attack. Devourer. Stealth. Oppression. Fear. Spiritual rebellion.

53. **Spiders** – Occult, people in the occult arena against you. Caught in a trap or web of lies. Bitterness.

54. **Squirrel-**Hoarder, accumulator and stasher. Squirrely thoughts confuses.

55. **Sharks** – Taking your peace.

56. **Snake** – Religious spirit. A long tail, someone is telling a 'tale' about you. Short tail, gossip. **Python** – constriction, diving spirit means to control. **Cobra** – Only focuses on world desire, represents a Pharaoh spirit of ruling control. **Rattler** – rattles makes noise causing confusion. **Black** – eats the other snakes. **Copperhead** – secret attacks against you. Snake bite to the heal – spirit of death. **Rat snake** – scary but not dangerous.

57. **Tiger-** Powerful predator, someone in ministry good or bad. Ruler and holding authority, Intimidating.

58. **Turkeys** – Wisdom or foolishness

59. **Turtles** – Peace. Slow pace. Steadfastness.

60. **Unicorn** – Resurrection power.

61. **Wasp-** Stinging lies or words. Witchcraft.

62. **Wolves** – False ministers.

63. **Worms** – Old thoughts "wormy", manna.

# 2
# ACTIVITIES

1. **Anointing-** Given the unction to serve by the Holy Spirit.
2. **Baptizing-**Washing away the old nature, covenant by water with God.
3. **Bathing-**Cleansing, washing. Purification.
4. **Bowing-** Humility, honor, tradition of a servant.
5. **Breathing-**Taking in the Spirit. Life giving. Breath of God.
6. **Eating or Banqueting-** Feasting. Partaking of the Lord's bountiful provision. Receiving the Word.
7. **Circumcising-** cutting away the carnal nature. Covenant seal. Religious traditions in law.
8. **Crying** – Sorrow, repentance. Soul cleansing.
9. **Dancing-** Joy, worship.
10. **Dreaming That You Are Dreaming** – Your destiny, things that God doesn't want you to miss.
11. **Dressing** – Note the color of the garment, if you are putting garment on, or taking garment

off.  (see objects)

12. **Eating** – Fellowship, covenant, provision. Partaking with the Lord (he that eats with Me....John 13:18)

13. **Falling** – Losing control, no support. Financial, or moral.  Falling away from the things of God.

14. **Fishing** – Evangelizing (fishers of men Matt. 4:19).

15. **Flying** – High spiritual activity God is taking you

16. **Fornicating**-Defilement, need deliverance from sexual spirit, adultery. Idolatry.

17. **Gardening** – Field of pleasant labor in ministry.  Bringing up the 'little seedlings'. Plowing new ground.

18. **Kiss/Kissing** – A covenant.  Neg. – a covenant breaker (Judas).  Seduction. Deception.

19. **Kneeling**- intercession

20. **Naked** – You have made yourself transparent before people.

21. **Running** – Legs don't work; something in your spirit is not operating yet.  Running away or towards.  Strife, anxiety.  To hurry (1Cor. 9:24).

22. **Running In Slow Motion** – Your spiritual walk.

23. **Running fast**- zeal for life. Running away

from a situation. Escape.

24. **Sitting in Chair**. resting in labor. Kind of chair- indicates a call on our life.

25. **Sleeping**-Spiritual indifference, resting, asleep as in physical death.

26. **Sweating**- fear strife, human effort.

27. **Swimming** – Operating in the gifts of the Spirit. Prophesying.

28. **Under Water But Not Drowning** – Deep spiritual things of God.

# 3
# COLORS

1. **Amber** – Holy. The Throne of God. God is ministering the anointing of fire.
2. **Black** –When representing the "bride" can be good as Solomon's bride was black. Can be evil, darkness, void. Dryness, sin and death.
3. **Blue** – The color of the prophetic. The color of heaven. Looking up to the Heavenlies, the sky is blue. The sea before the throne in Heaven. Communion, heavenly revelation. Depression, blues, hopelessness.(Neg.)
4. **Brown** – Servant, meekness, humility. Compassion, servitude, pastoral care. Dried out(Neg.)
5. **Gold** – The color of God's glory. Golden lam stands. Golden nuggets of wisdom from the 'gold mind'.
6. **Green** – Priestly, the color of teaching. A renewal, like spring grass. In someone's hands a gift of teaching. Prosperity. Growth Neg. – Inexperienced "He's green". Envy and jealousy.

7. **Grey** – Your grey matter, your thoughts not God's. A mixture, not very pure in color. A grey situation. Dismal. Lack of color (not of the Lord). Also ashy grey as in death. Ashy horse (Rev. 6:8).

8. **Indigo**-Knowledge

9. **Orange** – The sweet companionship of the Lord. Like a sweet orange. "Son Kissed".

10. **Purple** – The color of royalty (royal robes). Is a mixture of Red and Blue so represents revelation of the Blood. In someone's hands a gift of intercession. Authority, rule. Kingship. False authority(Jezebel)

11. **Red** – The Blood of Christ. Passion, love, fire, emotions, anger, lust. Red horse (Rev. 6:4) No peace. War. Bloodshed.

12. **Silver** – Righteousness (the tongue of the righteous is choice silver). The price of a soul's redemption (Ex. 30:11, Rev. 21:10). Sanctification.

13. **Violet**-Fear of the Lord

14. **White** – Purity, righteousness. White horse is Holy Spirit (Rev. 6:2). No blame, innocent.

15. **Yellow**-understanding, mind, and hope, courage, fear, and deceit.

# 4
# NUMBERS

1. **ONE** – Unity. The primary one. God Himself. The beginning. Unity. Eternal God. Independence.

2. **TWO** – Testimony of the two witnesses. Multiplication and increase. Division, separation, and difference.

3. **THREE** – Trinity. Perfect testimony. Power of agreement (3 strand cord, hard to break). Fellowship. Unity. Coordination. Perfection. Life.

4. **FOUR** – Number of the Holy Spirit. Four winds, four seasons, four directions. Creative works on the earth. (pos)weakness of mankind.

5. **FIVE** – Grace, atonement, life. Five fold ministry. God's favor. Redemption.

6. **SIX** – Number of man (man was created on sixth day). Number of the beast in Revelation. God's greatest creation, man. The weakness of man. Humanity and it's weakness.

7. **SEVEN** – Spiritual perfection. Completeness. Sanctification (Levitical priest). Seven gifts of the Holy Spirit. Seven Trumpets. Seven promises to the churches. Seven seals. Seven mysteries or secrets. Seven Spirits of God. Etc. God's number

8. **EIGHT** – Number of new beginnings. Resurrection, regeneration. The beginning of a new age and order. In Hebrew the number eight means "to cover with fat, to abound, to be fertile."

9. **NINE** – The completeness or conclusion of a matter. The fullness. The fruit of the Spirit. Number of fruit of the womb.(nine months) Finality. Tribulation

10. **TEN** – Number of law, order, government, restoration and anti-Christ kingdom. Divine order of God. Ten commandments. Wilderness. Pastor.

11. **ELEVEN** –Mercy, revelation, understanding and the prophets.(pos.) Imperfection, disorder, judgement. (neg)

12. **TWELVE** – Divine government, perfection and authority.

13. **THIRTEEN** – Rebellion, depravity.

14. **FOURTEEN** – Deliverance, release. Number of Passover.

15. **FIFTEEN** – New direction. Moving from a carnal walk, to a Godly walk.

16. **EIGHTEEN** – Oppression, bondage.
17. **TWENTY FOUR** – Heavenly government (twenty four elders).
18. **THIRTY** – Maturity and consecration to ministry.
19. **FORTY** – Judgment. Testing may end in victory or defeat.
20. **FIFTY** – Jubilee, freedom, liberty. Pentecost.
21. **SEVENTY** – Number of no turning back.
22. **SEVENTY-FIVE**- Separation, time of purification.
23. **Six-Six-Six**- Mark of the antichrist, satan, mark of the man that is the beast.

# 5
# MODES OF
# TRANSPORATION

Often vehicles will represent your ministry and relationship with God. The place we find our self in in the vehicle may represent our current activity within our ministry or someone else's.
Consider the vehicle and ask these questions to help you understand the dream.
Where am I in this vehicle? How fast am I going? Does this vehicle go on land, sea or in the air. Does it have tires or travel by railways. Is it on a road or small path? Am I driving or am I being driven? Is this vehicle real or imaginary? Is this vehicle in the future or in the past?

24. **Airplane** – Flying in the Spirit. If you are the pilot, you are pulling people with you, with Holy Spirit in control. You are soaring in the Spirit.

25. **Bicycle** – Walk out everything on your own in your ministry.

26. **Boats** – **Aircraft Carrier** – able to launch those filled with the Holy Spirit into their destiny. **Destroyer** – huge ministry, well equipped for battle. Launches major attacks on the enemy through worship (War-ship, Worship). **Sailboat** – Can only move by the winds of the Holy Spirit. Note if it's moving or still. **Fishing boat** – Evangelistic ministry, note size of boat. **Tugboat** – Intercessory ministry, pulling along the people of God through prayer.

27. **Bus** – Larger ministry with enough people to need 'bus size'.

28. **Car** – Personal ministry – what you are moving in. Note color and size, model and make.

29. **Chariot** – Place of God. Destiny. Something you are going to accomplish.

30. **Covered Wagon**- Trailblazing. Covered of God. A pioneer. An inheritance of ministry.

31. **Hot Air Balloon** – Free flowing in the Holy Spirit.

32. **Horseback**-riding on the back of the Holy Spirit. Powerful individual ministry.

33. **Military Tank** – Pushes the enemy back.

34. **Submarine**- Deep ministry of the spirit. Undercover of the deep waters of the Holy Spirit. Intercession.

35. **Truck** – Heavy duty, ready for

construction, for hauling. Also denotes a heavy duty, ready for battle, ministry. Note size and any signage on truck.

36. **Train** – Glory train. Are you a passenger or the engineer? Note color of train and any destination signage along the way. Passengers could be part of your ministry. United churches for same good purpose. Training center.

37. **Van**- group or home meetings

# 6
# OBJECTS

Objects will mean different things to the individual dreamer so try to understand what they mean to you. You may ask yourself what is the function of this object? If you own such an object what significance does it have to you? Is it inherited, is it lost? Is it old or something newly acquired? These are guidelines to get you started to understand what an object may mean in the Bible.

1. **Amethyst stone-** symbol of the royal priesthood.
2. **Altar** – Place of sacrifice (Ex. 27:1-8; Rev. 6:9).
3. **Anchor** – Our security. A place of stability
4. **Ant-** Symbol of wisdom. Good stewardship. Preparing diligently.
5. **Armor** – Armor of God. **Shield** – faith. **Helmet** – salvation. **Belt** – truth. **Shoes** – peace. **Sword** – Holy Spirit. Neg. – hole in the armor lets fiery darts in. Missing parts of the armor will denote where attacks will enter.

Where fortification is needed.

6. **Army-** Strong spiritual strength
7. **Aloe**- Healing from fire.
8. **Almond**-First fruit. Priest. New fresh beginning. Watchfulness. Awake, first blooming tree after a long winter.
9. **Apple blossom**- promises good health. Spring awakening. Tranquil and peaceful spirit
10. **Arrow**-spiritual attack, swift sure judgments.
11. **Ashes** – Repentance (Job 42:6).Destruction. Sorrow. Consumed in the fire.
12. **Atom Bomb** – Holy spirit outpouring. Sign of the last days. Miracles, power.
13. **Attic** – Old memories. Things on a shelves in an attic – things stored in your memory, it's time to take them off and either use them or get rid of them for good, depending on positive or negative meaning. Stored gifts not being used.
14. **Axe** – Word, the gospel. Also cutting away ('every tree that doesn't bring forth good fruit will be cut down. Matt. 3:10). Instrument for work (Isa. 10:15).Judgement. To cut.
15. **Babylon** – Confusion.
16. **Back Porch**- Old memories, back history.
17. **Bahamas** – Occult (Bermuda triangle). If a storm originates in the Bahamas – it's an attack of the enemy.
18. **Bakery**-A place of sweets. Pleasant words given. Righteousness being tried in the fiery

oven. The rewards the sweetness of salvation of the soul.

19. **Balm** – healing ministry (Jer. 8:22).

20. **Baldness**- no covering. Humility and weakness.

21. **Bands** around the wrists – covenant.

22. **Banks-** you make a withdrawal, something is going to cost you. You make deposits-something is about to be added to you.

23. **Banana-**gentle sweetness.

24. **Banner** – The tribes of Israel carried banners into war with their 'tribe name' written on the banner. If a banner has a name written on it, it could be telling you what warfare you are entering into, the area to be claimed. Can denote the identity of your tribe. Love (His banner over me is love.)

25. **Banquet Table** – our gifts from god that we may serve others. Provision. Resting and dining on the Lord's goodness. Kingdom of God is a banquet. To be blessed. All invited the lame and poor.

26. **Barns**- Storehouse. Supplies. Provision.

27. **Banner-** High standard. Covering. Love banner of Jesus.

28. **Basement** – below the surface or something hidden or partially hidden.

29. **Basket**-Provision

30. **Bathroom** – Prayer closet. Place of cleansing.

31. **Beam**- strength and support
32. **Bed** – Covenant, rest, salvation, peace and rest (Ps. 41:3)
33. **Bedroom**- a place to rest and recover.
34. **Belts** – Righteousness, Faithfulness, bound to service
35. **Bell**- Sweet sound. Worship.
36. **Bethel** – Place of God. Place of devotion.
37. **Beulah** – Married to the Lord. Owned and protected by the Lord.
38. **Birdbath** – Cleansing of demonic and confusion.
39. **Blemish**- imperfection of human nature
40. **Book-** History, Bible, knowledge.
41. **Bouquet of Flowers-** favor, and grace. A coming together of gifts. Note colors and types of flowers,
42. **Brass** –Judgment. Strength and endurance.
43. **Bread** – Bread of life (Jesus is bread of life John 6:35), sustenance, provision. Word of God. Manna from Heaven. New fresh word fro Heaven. Hot bread- comforting word.
44. **Bridge** – Holy spirit. The bridge between us and Jesus. Show transition from one place to another. Note color of bridge (see colors) for more in-depth meaning. Note what the bridge is 'bridging over'.
45. **Broom** – Sweeping away of the old. Cleaning out your spiritual or natural house.

46. **Bricks** – Works of man, made by man. Imprisonment, bondage (Egypt). Human works (Tower of Babel).

47. **Buildings** –Attic, thoughts. Basement, the "base nature(carnal). Note foundation. Cracks? Something cracked in your foundation-emotional or spiritual issues in your life. Church building, cracks in foundation? Can apply to any building etc.

Is there someone there, what are they doing, good or bad. Where are they in the building? Is there a good foundation, or are there cracks.     Is there an attic.(Old memories) Note type of building.    Office building – administration, being taken to a new office, new anointing. Work place- dealing with communication or interaction with others. A new "work".   High rise – level of calling, where you are going in your calling (medical building, healing anointing). Apartments where many dwell in separate areas. A community of people joined into one but in separate dwelling places. Separate Kingdoms. Separate ideas. Etc.

48. **Cedar** – The tree of royalty (1 Kings 9:11). A cedar chest where hope dwells(hope chest). Royalty. Strength. Power.

49. **Cake**-a sweet treat to eat...a good word. A

delicacy. Self indulgence. Need to use some self-restraint.

50. **Chain-** Binding up. Oppression and bondage.

51. **Chair** – A place of rest or a place of authority. A position you are in, your occupation or ministry. What kind of chair? Kingly chair or businessman's chair – position of authority.

52. **Chariot** – a place of God. If you're riding in the chariot, denotes your moving in your mantling (Elisha moved in his mantling when he saw Elijah leave in the chariot).

53. **Chocolate-** self-reward. Too much excess. Romance and gifts of friendship. Comfort.

54. **Church-**Fellowship. Community. Body of Christ.

55. **Cinnamon-** A fragrance of the Lord.

56. **Circle** – God, no beginning or end.

57. **City** – Will show you circumstances in your life. Security(refuge)

58. **Clay-** human flesh frailty

59. **Clock** – Time. God is saying; "It's TIME!" 12:00 – time for action, middle of the day, season or road. On a digital clock may refer to a scripture reference (11:11, Isa. 11:11). Counter clockwise

60. **Closet** – Your secret place. Your prayer closet. Hidden secrets. Aloneness.

61. **Clothing** – covering. Dirty clothes – unrighteousness. Dressed in white –

righteousness. Dressed in colors – note color (see Colors). Coat – mantle or anointing. Protection from elements, insulating you from 'things'. Cultural clothing – indicates where you are or who you may be ministering to. Invite to go to minister in that culture.

62. **Cluster of Grapes** – Group of believers together. Grapes (fruit of the Jesus the True Vine).

63. **Coal**-Burning fire, purification

64. **Cobblestone streets** – England or U.K. or quaintness and gentleness of time.

65. **Cocoon** – Protection of the Lord. Metamorphosis. The waiting room brfoe major change.

66. **College-** Learning higher spiritual things.

67. **Copper** – Conductor of power. Insulate.

68. **Corn**-Harvest. Die to self. Barns full. Increase of provision.

69. **Cornucopia** – Horn of plenty. Abundance. Blessed of the Lord. Promise for abundance. Note what its filled with. Fruit of the Spirit.

70. **Computer** – Your mind. Your analytical self. Information. Knowledge.

71. **Court**-Place of judgment and justice. Place of major decisions. Place where the rule of law is upheld.

72. **Crops**-harvest, seasons, your fruit.

73. **Crown** – Crown of salvation. Kingly power or

authority. Glory.

74. **Cup-** A full and running over cup. Great provision. Empty cup trials.

75. **Darkness** and all that is associated with darkness – sin and ignorance. Without Light.

76. **Darts** – attack (fiery darts). Hurtful words to amuse.

77. **Deaf-** Unable to hear. Physically or spiritually.

78. **Desert** – Barren, dry. A spiritual dry place. Could be a place to hear the Father's voice as Jesus went into the desert to pray. Observe circumstances and your other surroundings.

79. **Dining Room-** Place of fellowship with family and spiritual nourishment.

80. **Door** – New opportunity in Christ or from one from Him. An entrance into another place. An invitation to move.

81. **Door in Heaven-**Access to Heavenly places.

82. **Dragon** – Evil spirit with power. Destructive fire. Ancient demonic.

83. **Drugs** – Addiction. Influence, witchcraft. Medicine and healing.

84. **Dust** – Inactivity or neglect. Humiliation.

85. **Egg** – A beginning. New birth (life comes from an egg). Fresh start. Time of incubation for a new season. Caring for young, nurturing mother. Protecting the young.

86. **Egypt** – Bondage, slavery. Greed. Double suffering.

87. **Electricity** – Power (Holy Spirit is power), Lightning bolts are similar to this.
88. **Elevators** – Fast way up. Fast way to transition from one level to another.
89. **Emerald** - Glory of God
90. **Ephod** – Divine council.
91. **Ephraim** – Fruitfulness.
92. **Feathers** – Covering, Holy Spirit ("He shall cover you with His feathers" Ps. 91:4)
93. **Fire** - Holy Spirit, fire of the trials, new anointing, the angels are messengers of fire. A burning away of the old. A refining fire.
94. **Fountain** – Fountain of Life. Understanding. Fountain of living waters (Jer. 2:13). The Holy spirit. Three tiered fountain – Trinity.
95. **Fence** – Boundaries – in the spirit or in the natural. Religious doctrines, traditions. Note what is happening; breaking down boundaries or building up the defenses or fortresses.
96. **Footstool** – Stepping up and using something as your footstool (Ps. 110:1). A place to rest your feet on your walk.
97. **Field** - Symbol of the world. The harvest. Your place of ministry or sphere of influence.
98. **Fig** - fruit of Israel.
99. **Fire** – The Word in your mouth (Jer. 23:29). Passion, intense, heat, burning away of the old. The passion of the Lord, His Glory on the Throne. Burning up the dross in your soul.

Destructive fire in your circumstances or fire of the Holy Spirit, new infilling

100. **Flowers** – The fruit of the plant. Opening up. Glory. A sign of a new beginning. The flower blooms – then gives seed. Grace. Beauty. People flourishing. Withered flowers, doubt, disappointment, need of some "water".

101. **Food** – Foundational truth from the Word of God, type of food represents level of maturity, meat or milk. Bountiful provision. Apple- good health. **Orange**- sunshine or Son Shine. Pear tree- long fruitfulness. **Strawberries**- full of sweetened and lots of seed- fruitfulness. **Banana**- full of potassium- good for a health heart. Etc. Think of what you know about the fruit or any object always from it's symbolic message to you.

102. **Fountain-** the life source. Three tiers, Father. Son and Holy Spirit.

103. **Floor**- the earth. The foundation. The world

104. **Forest** – Thick and dense, darkness or confusion. Sometimes a place of protection. A forest of Cedars is great covering. Unable to see fully (I can't see the forest for the trees). Note context of the dream. Surrounded by leaders.

105. **Fortress** – Salvation. That which protects you and keeps the enemy out (Ps. 61:3).

106. **Front Porch**- your future. Place of rest.

Fellowship. Welcome.

107. **Furnace-** Symbol of trials. Fiery furnace of affliction.

108. **Garden** – The Church. Your field of labor. Your heart. Your soul. Jesus tends His garden…your soul. A place of visitation from the Lord. Fertile garden? Well watered garden.(watering by the Word) Dry garden, unfruitful, needs the water of the Holy Spirit. What are you doing in your garden. Plowing?(making hearts ready too receive the Lord)Harvesting(evangelizing)Watering?(teaching) Resting?(taking time with the Lord) Transplanting? Etc.

109. **Gate**- The entrance to the Heavens. An opening to the soul.

110. **Girdle**- committed to serve.

111. **Gold** – Glory. Gold on the lips – pure word of the Lord. Gold on the face – covered and mantled with His Glory. Gold on different body parts may indicate what the Lord is anointing at the moment. Nose (discernment) mouth or lips (spoken word out of your mouth) ears(what is heard) etc.

112. **Gold Jewelry** – Heart pendant around neck understanding and the heart of Jesus. Bracelets on each wrist – discretion. Nose ornament – discernment. Rings – ability to communicate. Necklace – fear of the Lord.

113. **Gilgal** – Place of dedication.
114. **Grapes**- faithfulness. Grapes of Wrath. New wine.
115. **Grass** – Humanity. Freshness of spring. Harvest.
116. **Gun** – If you're holding it – Dunamis power, dynamite in the Spirit. **Cap gun** – small, toy gun, lots of noise with no power. **Shotgun** – shoots your soul full of holes or the enemy full of holes. **Silver bullet in gun** – killing the enemy with the Word of God. Powerful words shot from a long distance(neg.)
117. **Hammer** – Word of God. To pound.
118. **Harp**- Praise and worship to God.
119. **Hay-** worthless stubble
120. **Hedge-** Protection. Boundary. Restricting movement
121. **Highway** – The way to get somewhere. Road of life. The truth. The way of life. If road splits – decision time. Narrow path – way of holiness. Dead end – time to look again, stop where you are, turn around and take the better road. Highway of Holiness.
122. **Hills**- Place of elevation. Some loftiness
123. **Honey** – Sweetness. Strength. Power by the Holy Spirit. God experience. The Lord see you as sweet unto Him.
124. **Horns** – Authority, power, anointing. The righteous (Ps. 75:10).

125. **Hospital** – A place of healing.

126. **Hot air Balloon** – A peaceful rising in the Spirit.

127. **House** – House of the Lord. That which you are comfortable in, you have made this house your home, where you reside. In disarray? Places that in dreamers life need cleaned up or simplified or organized. Childhood homes may indicate a need for resolving old issues in your life.

128. **Hyssop**- symbol of healing Purification.

129. **Iceland** – What happens here is what the Lord is doing.

130. **Iron** – Imprisoned. Chains. Relationship, iron sharpens iron.

131. **Jericho** – A place of discipline. Waiting till the time is right.

132. **Jewels**-anointing, wealth and favor, inheritance, pleasure, gifts, special seasons, gifts from the King.

133. **Jordon** – Baptism in the Holy Spirit. Place of declaring God is you Savior. Healing. Redemption.

134. **Key** – Keys open doors of wisdom and knowledge, and opportunity. Open prison doors. Given to those in authority to begin a new thing.

135. **Keys To City** – God's hand is there.

136. **Kitchen-** Place to prepare spiritual food.

137. **Knives** – Sharp truth, or anger with words. Revelation. Cutting away. Stab in the back.

138. **Ladder** – where you go up or come down (Jacob's ladder). Open heaven. Son of Man connecting heaven to earth (Gen. 28:12, John 1:51).

139. **Lamps**-Spirit of Man. Light for your feet.

140. **Lakes** – still bodies of water speaks of not moving in the 'River of God'. Comfortable where you are.

141. **Leaves** – Healing for the nations. Covering yourself with fig leaves, temporary hiding from the Lord (Adam and Eve). Falling leaves – a late season like autumn. Hopelessness. Loss. Withered or dry, hope deferred. Forsake or abandon.

142. **Leaven-**doctrines of man. Pharisees.

143. **Lemon-**sour thoughts or words.

144. **Mall –** marketplace. Community provision.

145. **Marble-** Kingdom elegance and beauty

146. **Manna-** Heavenly bread or heavenly revelation. Fresh manna best. Wormy manna, old thoughts and attitudes.

147. **Map** – Direction. Note direction on the map. Note cities or particular places on the map.

148. **Maze** – Walking outside of the Spirit. Walking in confusion and uncertainty.

149. **Meat**- The strong food, or Word.

150. **Milk**- Milk of the Word. Not ready yet for the Meat of the Word.

151. **Mirror**- image, what you may really look like. Image of God, reflection of God.

152. **Money** – Natural or spiritual provision. The trusting of man's power over God's power.(neg) The increase or decrease of favor with man. Provision or lack of provision. **CHANGE**-(Nickels and dimes) making change in a dream you will be making a change in life. Pennys-widows mite.

153. **Monsters** – demonic. White monsters appear to be Holy but are destructive. Religious spirit. Demonic as angels of light.

154. **Moon** – Bride of Christ. Reflection of the son. Golden moon great harvest. Blue moon great revelation about to be revealed. Negative is witchcraft and control. Sign of the Son of Man.

155. **Net**- A catcher, an evangelist.

156. **Newspaper** – Important current up to date announcement, good or bad.

157. **Night**- Spiritual darkness. A time of Dark night of the soul. A tribulation.

158. **North** – Evil comes out of the north.

159. **Oak**- Righteousness, truth. Leadership. Meeting place for the angels. Young prophets sat under. Burn offerings under. Acorns are increased fruitfulness.

160. **Oil** – Anointing, healing. That which greases the move of the Spirit (oil in an car). Oil that moves your ministry.

161. **Pasture**- A resting and provision place.

162. **Palm Tree**- Place of rulership and judgment.(Deborah) Victory. A place of rest.

163. **Pearl** – Great suffering. Great price. Giving everything up for Jesus.

164. **Pillar** – What is established and sure from God. Stability. Firm support.

165. **Pitcher**- Humankind ready to be filled. A earthen vessel.

166. **Platter** – Lots of spiritual food coming.

167. **Pots or Pans** – Vessels. God's vessel's ready to be filled (clay pots).

168. **Red Sea** – Escape from bondage. Miracles. Destruction of the enemy. Faith.

169. **Restaurant**-Fellowship, spiritual food.

170. **Ribbons** – Reminders, note colors (see colors), note what they are tied to. Gifts from God.

171. **Rings**- Authority. Covenant

172. **River** – River of the Spirit. Where the Spirit flows. Cleansing. Rivers of living waters (John 7:37-39).

173. **Rod**- Shepherding. Priesthood. Guidance.

174. **Roses**- red=love. Pink sweetness innocence, yellow=loss of love, infidelity, gladness, friendship, white= purity and innocence.

175. **Rubies** – great rarity and wealth, highly prized. Wisdom, a virtuous wife, lips full of knowledge.

176. **Salt** – Biblical symbol of permanence of covenant between God and His people. Purification.

177. **Sapphires**-tests which refine a person, true or divine judgments, revelatory gift.

178. **Schools** – Places of education. A place where test are passed or failed. A place of re-testing.

179. **Shower** in Bathroom washing by the Word. Cleansing

180. **Seed** – Word of God. That which you plant expecting good fruit. Seed that is good or bad. A new beginning. A new harvest. A new work. The essence of it. Faith, abundance or lack of it (the grain of a mustard see).

181. **Silver-** redemption. Slavery. Knowledge. Settings of Silver-fine words.

182. **Skins-** A covering.

183. **Smoke-** A covering up of something.

184. **Spices-** Sufferings, fragrance by crushing. Offerings to the Lord.

185. **Sword** – Word of the Spirit. That which is the Lord's to cut away or edify. Two edge sword. Stabbing words.

186. **Smoke** – His Glory. His manifest presence. The saint's prayers as incense. God's judgment

is manifest in smoke (Sodom and Gomorrah, Gen. 19:28).

187. **Soap**- Cleansing.

188. **Sour-** A "bad taste in mouth" over an issue. False teaching, another "bad taste in your mouth"

189. **Stars** – Angels of churches (Rev. 9:20). Abrahams seed. Ministers of the gospel. Spiritual Israel.

190. **Stone**- spiritual truths, stubbornness(set in stone) white stone(new name.) Stability of Christ the "Rock".

191. **Sun** – Jesus, the Light of the World. The protection, the heat. "For the Lord God is a sun and a shield." Ps. 84:11. Glory.

192. **Swimming Pool** – Your spiritual place or your spiritual condition. Good or bad. Healing pools of Bethesda. A place of healing.

193. **Tares**- weeds in the garden, bad things that cause distraction, sin in lives, false appearing real, poisonous thoughts that will ruin the good. False teaching.

194. **Tea** – Good news. Refreshment from the Lord. Stimuli from the Lord to move. Teaching, sweet teaching. "Tea time," rest of the Lord.

195. **Tears** – Sorrow, repentance. Tears of Joy. Cleansing the soul.

196. **Teeth** – Chewing of the Word. Loosing

teeth – inability to understand the Word. Eye teeth – prophetic. Incisors – speak of decision. Wisdom teeth – wisdom. Sharpness and devouring.

197. **Telephone-** Communication. Cell phone to Abba. Praying in the Spirit.

198. **Thorns** – Distraction or hindrance or reminders. The curse. Persecution. Miner fuss or disturbance. Punishment, twisted and entangled.

199. **Tomato** – A fully seeded fruit full of nutrition. A big heart.

200. **Trees** – Genealogy, curses or blessings. Family trees. Trees of righteousness (Ezekiel 17:24). A shelter. Note the different types of tree and color of leaves, what season etc. for further interpretation. We are the tree.

201. **Trumpet** – The clear trumpet, the clear voice, the true prophet. The clear warning. What color is the trumpet?

202. **Veil**- Separates us from God.

203. **Wall-** Separation, Security. Protection.

204. **Water** – Holy Spirit. Oceans – sea of humanity.

205. **Warehouses-** Abundant provision.

206. **Well-** A place to be watered. A deep sourse of water. Drawing out of the well, receiving water of life.

207. **Wheat-** Increase and multiplication. Harvest.

208. **Wheel Barrow** (3 wheel) – Trinity. Trust.

209. **Weights-** a burden, heavy life circumstances.

210. **Wilderness-** A place to hear God's voice. A place prepared by God to take His people in a season. A place of preparation for the next season.

211. **Willow tree.** A sorrowful place. Weeping in repentance. Deep roots seeking water.

212. **Window** – Revelation. Seeing into the Spirit. Truth. Portals into the revelatory realm. Windows open and the blessings come in. Open windows shed light on darkness.

213. **Wine-** Joy and sweet teaching. New wine and new teaching and revelation from the Lord. Drunkenness' in the spirit. To complain(whine)

214. **Wood, Hay and Stubble** – Works of the flesh. Things done for self-glory. Non-decaying wood.

215. **Wooden Raft** – A way out of a storm, but has 'gaps' in the Spirit.

216. **Yeast-** Leaven-doctrines of man.

# 7
# PEOPLE / BODY PARTS

Consider these possibilities: Do I know this person and what do they represent to me? What does the person's name mean? How would I describe this person? Is this a positive or negative person? What relationship does this person have to me?

By understanding what a particular body part function in the body is we will know why they have been shown in a dream.

1. **A Best Friend** – Could represent Jesus.
2. **Angels** – Interpreting Angels. Messenger angels. Ministering spirits for the saints of God. Angels of God will be – light and bright. Will speak the messages of God. Neg. Satan comes disguised as an angel of light, he has light, but its dark light.
3. **Beard**- Priestly beard, wisdom and age.
4. **Bride** – Bride of Christ. Something you are intimately joined to. An upcoming "marriage" of a company or and close union in business or personal.
5. **Boss**- authority, neg. or pos.
6. **Brother** – May represent Jesus. Your

biological brother or your brother in the faith.

7. **Children/babies**-A new beginning. A new season. Child like. Dependency. Innocence. Purity. Naivety. Spiritual fruit. Needing to "mature".

8. **Demons** – terrifying spirits who come to terrify. Servants of satan carrying out his orders to kill, steal and destroy. Sometimes appear as Roman Soldiers, gargoyles. Are always dark and lack color and light.

9. **Ederly**- Wisdom, Ancient of Days, Jesus, Holy Spirit. Also weakness.

10. **Faceless Man** – Holy Spirit.

11. **Father**-Provider. Abba, comfort and fatherly wisdom.

12. **Kings** – An apostolic calling.

13. **Moses** – Government

14. **Mother**-church. Nurturer or spiritual mother comforter.

15. **Pastor** – Becoming pastoral, a calling dream. Counsel from the Father's heart.

16. **President or Leader of a Nation** – Represents someone in great authority, could be the Lord.

17. **Prophet** – Prophetic Word God is bringing to you.

18. **Prostitute**-the false church. Sexual idolatry.

19. **Tongue**-Blessing or cursing. Power of

speech.

20. **Famous people**- what do they represent to you?
21. **Familiar People** – From God.
22. **Father** – Represents heart of Abba, Fatherly advice.
23. **Unfamiliar People** – Don't listen to them until you test the spirit.
24. **Woman** – May represent Church, depending on demeanor.
25. **Breath** – Impartation of life (God breathed breath of life into man).

26. **Breasts** – Mother in the Spirit. Comforting. Nurturing.
27. **Ears** – Ears to hear. Large ears – good discernment. Pierced ear – commitment to hear the Lord. Deaf ear – unable to hear the Lord. Channel to receive faith.
28. **Eyes** – Eyes to see. Color of eyes denotes gifts (blue – revelatory eyes). Clouded or Scales over eyes – Inability to see in the Spirit. Eyes are windows to the soul, they show the condition of the soul. Occult third eye, seduction.

29. **Feet** – Walking out your ministry. Bowing at His feet. Complete submission to the Lord. Neg. Running to evil (Isa. 59:7). Left Foot –

ministry now. Right Foot – faith for ministry now. Bring good news. Walking over people.(neg.) Evangelist. Tread on Scorpions(=witchcraft)

30. **Fingers** – **Thumb** – Apostolic, government. **Pointer** – Prophet, guide. **Middle Finger** – Evangelist, gatherer. **Fourth Finger** – Teacher, grounder. **Pinkie Finger** – Pastor, guard.

31. **Hair** – Covering (1 Cor. 11:15). Red hair – wisdom. Baldness – no covering or shame.Glory.

32. **Hands** – Service, ministry, worship. Right hand – hand of faith and a blessing yet to come, power of God. Left hand – ministry right now, this moment. Helping. Relationship. Serving.

33. **Head** – Brain and logical reasoning.

34. **Heel** – Crushing power, victory.

35. **Hip or Thigh** – commitment.

36. **Kidneys** – Where the anointing from. Where witchcraft hits.

37. **Knees** – Worship, adoration, and intercession.

38. **Lungs** – Congested lungs – unable to breath. in the Holy Spirit. Congestion or confusion, attack by enemy to steal your breath to speak.

39. **Legs**-Strength, commitment, support.

Pillars.

40. **Naked**-Transparent, vulnerable, unprepared. No covering, no guile. Sexual.

41. **Neck**- Stiff necked. Strength.

42. **Nose**-Discernment. Meddling. Nosey.

43. **Shoulder**- Burden bearer and government. Government.

# 8
# WEATHER/DIRECTIONS

1. **Breeze** – A gentle breeze is the still small voice.
2. **Black Clouds** – God hides Himself in the black clouds. Neg. Impending disaster.
3. **Blue skys**- revelation. Open Heaven. Heavenly understanding
4. **Drought** – A curse, no blessings. Waiting for the move of the Spirit.

5. **Down-** Spiritual backsliding. Humility. Demotion

6. **East-** Sun rising. Glory.
7. **Earthquake** – Natural or spiritual upheaval. Disaster and judgment. Shakings of God.
8. **Flooding** – Drenched in the Spirit. Drowned in sin or judgment. Temptation.
9. **Fog** – Confusion. Can't see clearly. Clouded thoughts. Clouded issues for decision making.
10. **Hail** – Hidden lies. Curse. Judgment from

God.

11. **Hurricanes** – Divine disturbances.

12. **Northern Lights** – Revealing the Son of God.

13. **North-**Judgments of God. Place of God's throne.

14. **South-** Place to be refreshed. Help comes from here.

15. **Thunder-** God's voice. God speaking.

16. **Tornado**- winds of change coming, note black or white tornado.

17. **Rain** – Blessings of the Holy Spirit. Brings life, waters the parched ground.

18. **Rainbow** – Covenant. Giftings. Heavenly Throne. Look at the colors and record them. The arc of God. Double Rainbows. Double anointing.

Sleet- Slippery way. Judgment. Danger to fall. Move with caution. Watch out for "black ice"

19. **Snow** – Righteousness or judgment. Winter season of life. Holiness. Abba covering in love. Purity.

20. **Tsunami** – Massive move of the Spirit. Massive move of destruction by the devil.

21. **Tornados** – Destruction. Dark, the enemy is coming to destroy. White, God could be coming to destroy.

22. **Up**- Up in spiritual things.

23. **West**- setting sun.

24. **Wind** – He will make His angels His winds. Winds of change. Spirit winds.
25. **Wind storm**- blowing away of the chaff. Windstorm of life a challenge coming. Facing the wind. A season of testing and trials.

Brenda McDonald is a gifted dream interpreter, international speaker, and ordained minister. Brenda moves in the seer and revelatory realm. Her heart is to see Jesus' Bride become fully equipped to move in the Spirit of Revelation knowledge of the Lord Jesus. She equips the Saints of God to move into the "ripe Harvest Field" with dream interpretation as an evangelistic tool. She has written numerous articles and teachings on our inherited authority, moving in God's power and understanding our dreams.

She has a love of God's people and a heart for the great Harvest of the lost.

**Other Books By Brenda McDonald:**

*"Dream Interpretations Guidelines Christian Dream Symbols"*

*"How Do You Know Me?"*

*"The Dream and The Torch"*

*"Seer Anointing"*

*Books available on Amazon and Kindle*

**For more information**
About Brenda McDonald
**www.Seer Anointing.com**

Made in the USA
Lexington, KY
29 July 2015